STRAIGHT FROM THE HEART

Monica Seales Thomas

STRAIGHT FROM THE HEART

By

Monica Seales Thomas

Published By
Eagles Word Christian Publisher
New York

Copyright © May 2024 by Monica Seales Thomas
All Rights Reserved.
ISBN:979-8-9878522-6-2

No part of this publication may be reproduced, stored in a retrieval system, or transmitted in any form or by any means, for example, electronic, photocopying, recording without prior written permission of the author. The only exception to this is brief quotations in printed reviews.

Unless otherwise indicated, all Scriptures quotations are taken from the English Standard Version of the Holy Bible

Printed in the United States of America

Dedication

This book of poems is dedicated to everyone who faces challenges that put limitations on who they are and what they can accomplish in life. Through these written words, I declare that you can do all things through Christ who gives you strength every day. Through God's grace you can finish your course, yes you can! Why? Because you have the faith and grace to do it all.

Acknowledgement

I want to extend my deepest love and thanks to my Lord and Savior, the One true God who is the Creator of heaven and earth. He is my all and all. He is the One who gives me the ability to write this book of poems.

I also extend my love and gratitude to my husband, Cecil Thomas, who has been with me through the journey of sleepless nights and early morning experiences. I love you for the patient husband you are—putting up with me through it all. Love you always.

To my sister, Pastor Veronica Whites who encouraged me to continue writing. When I had stopped, she said to me, "you will publish a book of heartfelt poems;" and that is how this masterpiece started. I love you, Sis.

A special thank you goes to Lourdes Lewin, my friend and sister in Christ. God placed you in my life at a time when I was lost—not knowing the Lord's purpose for me. You encourage me every day. You said to me, "you have all these poems—why don't you get them published? I will give you the name of my publisher, and we will take it from there.

A Father's Love

Have you ever wondered what it would feel like to have the love of your father?

As a child growing up, I always wanted the love of my father, but all I got was abuse! I often wondered what it would have felt like to be hugged by my father, to play games or do other things with my father, or maybe just to sit and talk. Instead of that, I experienced abuse, even though my mother was alive.

At ten years old my mother went to be with the Lord and that's when *all* hell broke loose. I thought that my father would have protected me from the world! Instead, I was left out there for anyone to do anything they desired to me. I used to ask myself what happened to the kind of love a father should have for his child or children? How could a father leave such innocence to be violated by anyone?

One thing is sure, however, and that is, that my Heavenly Father loves me. Having that knowledge is the reason I became the woman I am today; because He protected me from all the abuse.

Thank you, Heavenly Father, for loving me.

A Mother's Love

A mother's love is just like a security blanket; once you are inside of it you're safe and protected.

A mother's love bonds with her child or children; she is so gentle and loving, like a lioness protecting her cubs. She is always by your side to hug you, to love you and to kiss away your fears and pain.

One of the greatest loves you will ever find is a mother's love. Whenever you encounter that type of love, cherish it; because you will never have or find a love like a mother's love. Once it is gone you will never get it back.

That type of love has brought smiles and laughter, tears and pain.

I sometimes long for that type of love again where I can feel loved and protected.

Acceptance

You accept me when I mess up.
You accept me when I am not myself.
You accept me when other people turn away from me.
You accept me for who I am.
You accept me like the prodigal son.
You accept me with all my faults, all my ways,
and all my blemishes;
You accept me.
I love You for accepting me when I was not acceptable;
For teaching me how to love myself and how to love
others in an unacceptable world.

Thank you, Lord, for Your unconditional love,
acceptable throughout my life.

A Prayer For Faith and Power

Dear Lord, I believe with all my heart that You have an exciting purpose and plan for me. I want to live according to Your will, so I can experience Your power to overcome life's obstacles, and experience Your peace even in the middle of tough circumstances.

Help me to live with an attitude of faith and expectancy today, knowing that You want to do great things in my life and use me to bless others.

Give me a teachable spirit and the ability to stand strong in adversity. And give me a servant's heart that looks for ways to meet other people's needs.

Thank You for what you are doing to prepare me for a life of victory, abundance and blessing beyond anything I could ask or even imagine.

I pray all of this in the Name of Jesus Christ. Amen.

From Monica

Communication

We do not communicate anymore with the people who are among us and around us.

We sit in a church setting and sometimes the only thing we will say to our brothers and sisters is, 'good morning.' No other type of communication.

We do not even ask them how they are doing today or how their week was. Sometimes you may give them a complement by saying 'you're looking mighty fine today' or 'I like your hairstyle,' or 'do you need help with anything'?

Yet, we go to God, and we want to communicate with Him. The Lord says, 'if my people who are called by my name, will humble themselves and pray and seek my face and turn from their wicked ways, then I will hear from heaven, and I will forgive their sin and will heal their land.' (2 Chronicles: 7:14).

The Lord said, 'I put people among you so that you can communicate with them about my kingdom; still, there is no verbal communication. Instead, persons go on all social media platforms and communicate with people whom they don't even know.

People of God, a time will come when you won't be able to communicate with each other, so I ask you today to do more communicating with others around you. Communication is the key that unlocks great things for our lives, so let us start communicating with each other.

Prayer For Strength

Almighty Father of our Lord Jesus Christ

By whom the whole family in Heaven and earth is named

Grant us to be strong in might by His Spirit in the inner man

That through Christ, dwelling in our hearts and souls by faith, we will be filled with the fullness of Almighty God.

Empress

E	Empowered to
M	Maintain her
P	Personality with
R	Respect; to
E	Encourage and
S	Speak her mind with
S	Sovereignty to share with others

Expressing my True Self

Being true to myself is being willing to look
within my inner world.
Sometimes it can be like a walk in the woods,
turning over rocks, looking to see
what lies beneath them.
I may follow a bird's singing
and find that bird in the treetop.

My self-awareness and consciousness grounds me in the knowledge and understanding that making changes to outer things is not the key to an authentic life.

I must go deep within myself and continue to examine everything to determine the root from which everything stems. Looking inward and reconsidering my thoughts, my beliefs and habits continues to propel me toward greater exploration and discovery to find and express my true self.

Help Me Find My Way

Heavenly Father, as I come before Your throne today, I am asking You for Your help to find my way back to You.

A while back I lost my way after I became sick and didn't know what to do, or to whom to turn at that time.

I think of the people whom I thought would be by my side, but they were not there for me. What a shame that I put my trust in people and not in You, Lord!

Thank You for Your forgiveness, Your Love, Your mercy, and Your grace that You show me always. As I turn myself around and come back to You, the Comforter, to give me comfort in my time of adversity, I thank You for patiently waiting for me.

Humbleness

Father, as I humbly come before You today, as Your disciple in Your Kingdom, I thank You for Your faithfulness to Your people.

We thank You for everything You do for us on planet earth. You show us your love, peace, and mercies every day. (according to Deuteronomy 6:5 NIV *'Love the Lord your God with all your heart and with all your soul and with all your strength').*

So how can we show our love to the Lord today? We can intentionally spend time with God each day.

We can be obedient to God's directions in our lives today. We can act in ways that show others what God is like. We can show them how to find salvation in Christ.

I Am Centered

I am centered when I practice to align myself with the Divine nature; feeling peace, assurance, and a sense of being grounded.

I am centered when my heart is open fearlessly to what life brings to me, knowing that nothing can knock me off balance.

I will never need to look outside myself with worry or anxiety for rescue or provision; for when I am centered and open, I become aware of the spiritual guidance within, causing me to realize that everything good comes to me in wondrous ways.

All that I will ever need comes from the spiritual presence within me. As I pray and meditate, I center myself in the awareness of this eternal source of my life that brings me peace of mind and causes me to focus on what I have to do spiritually.

I Am Free

Like an eagle, I'm ready to fly away from the nest of my comfort zone; my desire is to soar higher and higher to reach my goals.

I was born free, created by my Heavenly Father in His image. At times I feel frustrated as I journey through life, but then I turn to Holy Spirit and remember my true nature.

When I feel stuck in some areas of my life, facing deep spiritual challenges, I will draw upon the power of Holy Spirit to free myself! By affirming my freedom, I re-claim my power by telling myself that I am powerful beyond measure! I am empowered to break the mental and emotional chains that have been holding me back as I choose to soar as an eagle through my life's journey.

I Am Grateful

I am grateful to You Lord, every day. You woke me up to see another day here on planet earth in the land of the living. I am grateful to You Lord for spared life.

I am grateful to You Lord for always providing for me.

I am grateful to You Lord for your forgiveness, Your mercy, Your love and Your grace toward me.

I am grateful to You Lord for the work of the Crucifixion, the work of the Resurrection and the work of the Ascension.

I am grateful to You Lord for comforting me in times of my adversity.

I am grateful to You Lord for shielding and protecting my family members and me each day.

I am grateful to You Lord for all Your love with which You surround my family and me; that love that we can share with others.

I am grateful to You Lord for every miracle You have done in my life.

Thank You Lord for Your graciousness towards me.

That's why, Lord, I am so grateful to You.

I Am Special in Jesus' Eyes

Lord, strengthen my mind, body and spirit when I am weary. Refresh me when I am exhausted and worn out — renew me. When I am broken, restore me. When I am afraid, may I be encouraged and strengthened by You.

Let me walk in complete confidence and faith knowing that You, Lord, are with me every step of the way.

I say Hallelujah unto You. Without You I am nothing; but in You I can do all things; knowing that I am the apple of Your eyes and You always keep watch over me.

Monica

M - for the mysteries inside me.

O - for overcoming life's obstacles.

N - for never holding back what's inside of me.

I - for the incredible things I can do.

C - for that caring heart within me.

A - for the ability to do all things I was created to do.

Together it means that God created me in a way that no one will ever understand.

Life

This life that we all live is wonderful
It begins with birth and ends with death.
What is beyond birth and death?

> *Majesty! Blessed Majesty!*
> *How fortunate for us*
> *that we have life!*
> *From eternity into*
> *a little space in time.*

We come into view and we pass out of view in a delightful and an everlasting succession of surprises, some call...*Amazing Grace!*

My Bleeding Heart

My bleeding heart hurts so much at times, that I cannot stop the blood from flowing;
The hurt and the pain that my heart endures!!

I often wonder why my heart must go through so much pain and suffering. I wish at times I could stop all the blood from flowing from my bleeding heart.

I only wish that people would stop hurting this loving heart of mine and try to embrace and cherish the love that this heart has to give and share with them.

Will I be able to stop this heart from bleeding so much? I am hoping that one day someone will come along and stop my heart from bleeding.

The Joy of Love

The joy of love is sorrow
The joy of love is pain
The joy of love is comforting
The joy of love is laughter
The joy of love is communication
The joy of love is understanding
The joy of love is the feeling that you have inside of you which you cannot explain
The joy of love is so deep that not everyone encounters it.

The joy of love is loving yourself and God at the same time.

The Love I Have Inside

There is a love inside of me
Which no one in my life seems to see
A love that is true, a love that is strong
A love that could last all life long.
The love that I have is good and clear
Not even my boyfriend seems to care—
The love that I have is so plain and bright
No one can see it in the darkest night.
I wish someone could only share
This love I've been holding all these years;
I wish someone could only see
The love that I have wrapped up in me.

Love Lifted Me Up Out of Darkness

I have a connection with a loving Father that can never be severed.

While carnal love can end, God's love is eternal. This love is part of my Divine nature. I am able to access God's love at every moment, regardless of where I am or what I am doing.

When I find myself feeling sad or discouraged, afraid or angry, I turn to the one present love that is always available to comfort me.

I can shift my focus from pain to love knowing that love is the foundation of all creation. In my darkest times I allow love to lift me up.

My Heart

My heart is a heart so full of love, it's pouring out from inside waiting for returned love.

Sometimes my heart hurts so much from lack of love, waiting on that special someone who will come along and give this heart of mine the love and care that it desires.

I once gave my heart to someone who did not care about my heart or all the love my heart had to give. My heart was stomped upon and left aching for that love.

I hope one day to find the right one to love who will love me in return, so that our hearts could beat as one.

I give my heart to love, my heart of peace, my heart of joy, my heart of forgiveness, my heart of sincerity, my heart of transformation and freedom to love again.

I Love You

I love you because
You make my life so wonderful.
I love you
More than words can say.
I love you
Just for being yourself.

I love you because
You showed me how wonderful life can be.
I love you in
So many ways that one could think of.

I love you
When you open up and let your guard down.
I love you
When we both get angry at each other.
I love you
When we both forgive each other.

But just remember, don't take my love for granted.
It's not because I love you, you're going
to break my heart.

My Inner Peace

As I turn within myself, I focus on my inner peace. In the worst of times I will slip away physically and mentally to be apart from the things that are going on around me.

When I feel that I am losing touch with my inner peace, I can turn within the garden of my heart — my sanctuary where peace resides.

Focusing on my breathing, I inhale peace, and I exhale love. I let these statements permeate my very being as I rest in the sanctuary of peace and love.

I will rise above stressful moments as I consciously connect with the Divine love that lives in me. This love is the power that lifts my spirits.

By taking in a few deep breaths I still my thoughts and let everything around me slip away to a place where I can connect with the Holy Spirit. In this place of oneness I find peace, forgiveness, love and faith.

As I let love wash over my soul, I can contribute in helping others find inner peace within their own selves.

Thank You

Thank you for being there for me.
Thank you for the kind words
You gave me.

Thank you for that smile you put
on my face.
Thank you for that hug which Comforted me.

Thank you for sharing in all of my sorrows and pain,
and my joy.
Thank you for the jokes that made
me laugh.

Thank you for holding my hand
through it all.

Thank you!

My Intimate Love with Jehovah

You are the light that shines
in my dark place
You are the music that I hear
that won't ever fade away
Your food is what I feed on,
which supplies everything that I need

You're a love like no other love
I will ever have or want
You're my pain-bearer when I am hurting
You're my eyes when I cannot see
You're my voice when I cannot speak
You're my feet when I cannot walk,
You'll lift me up and carry me.

You're my way maker when there's no way
You're my miracle worker,
working miracles for me

Your love for me will never die or fade away
It's an unconditional love that will live on
through eternity.

My Life's Ability

Now is the time and moment I answer my Divine calling and express the greatness of my soul. I am capable of every success in my life. I am destined to fulfill every mission.

Every day provides me with opportunities to improve myself and develop new skills to achieve new things.

As I exercise my God-centered courage to expand and grow beyond what is familiar and comfortable for me, my old habits and limits pass away; my fear dissolves, leaving behind no uncertainty.

I am nurtured and loved by the Spirit of Jehovah flowing in and through me, guiding me in every way — as His light shines upon my life to manifest my abilities — all for His glory.

Nothing is Impossible

Lord, nothing is impossible for You.
There is no sickness You cannot heal, no diseases You cannot cure; No fight You cannot win.
There is nothing impossible that you cannot do for me.

So right now, I am asking You Lord to protect me, strengthen me, heal and comfort me.

I need You to show up in my life and do what only You can do.

In Jesus' Almighty name.

Prayer

Father, in the name of Jesus Christ, Son of the living God, I thank You for the open doors of life, health, strength, prosperity, wealth, and love.

Also, I thank You for closing the doors of death, sickness, weakness, despair poverty and bitterness.

I love You today Lord, with all my heart, as I give unto You all the glory, all the honor and all the praise.

I seal this prayer in Jesus' Almighty name. Amen.

Promise Yourself

Promise yourself to be strong so that nothing can disturb your peace of mind.
To speak of good health, happiness, and prosperity to every person that you meet.
To make all your family and friends aware of the special qualities within them.
To look at the sunny side of everything and let your optimism work to make your dream come true.
To think, work and expect only the best.

To be just as enthusiastic about the success of others as you are about your own.
To forget past mistakes and press on towards a greater future.
To always wear a cheerful countenance, as a smile radiates warmth and love.

The improvement of yourself is giving of your time so that you have no time left to criticize others.
To be too wise to worry, too tolerant to anger and too courageous to fear.

Always be happy.

Rejection

Have you ever been rejected by people, family members, and close friends? Sometimes you ask yourself what did I do to all these people for them to reject me the way they do?

Today I come to encourage someone who is struggling with rejection, Do not give up! Your Creator loves you and will never reject you no matter what you have done in your life or what circumstances you may have gone through. Your Heavenly Father will never reject you!

Because He loves you unconditionally — a love you will not find anywhere or obtain from anyone. Anytime you feel rejected always remember that He is your Creator and loves and adores you. He will never blame you or reject you for your past mistakes or pretend to love you.

Loves comes freely and is unconditional.

Remind Yourself.

Remind yourself you are loved by God, and He forgives you of all your sins.

Remind yourself that when you were lost God found you. Remind yourself that you are a new creation. Remind yourself that you are empowered by the Spirit of God to walk in your new purpose in life.

Remind yourself that you will walk in God's truth; that He has purpose for your life! Remind yourself that you are precious in God's eyes.

Remind yourself that you are loved by God who sees you for who you are. Remind yourself you were created with the ability to prosper in your life!

Remind yourself of what you really want for your life. Remind yourself that God wants you to have a great life so you can be an example for Him.

Remind yourself that God planted seeds of greatness, uniqueness, and potential inside of you. Remind yourself that God masterfully made you and said that He will give you the desires of your heart if you only trust Him.

Remind yourself when you feel unworthy that you are worthy of God's love, that He sacrificed for you with His arms out-stretched wide.

Rose of Love

Love is like a rose, it's so beautiful.

Its petals are so perfectly put together and smell so sweet and wonderful.

You cannot resist cherishing and holding it in your hands, close to your heart, without being hurt by its thorn.

As beautiful as that rose is, it is also painful. One prick of its thorn and the pain shoots straight to your heart. With that one prick comes rage, pain with sorrow.

With all those emotions together, you will destroy that sweet-smelling rose which once seemed so beautiful. It is a pain you never expected.

That is what love can do to you also— just like that sweet smelling rose.

My Sister

My sister is extraordinary; she's one of a kind.
No one would ever come across another one like her.
When I speak about my sister it brings tears to my eyes.
My sister is loving, kindhearted, trustworthy,
and most of all, wise.

When I need someone to talk to, I look toward my sister.
I have learnt much from the advice she gives.
Sometimes when I am alone, I hear her voice
speaking to me. Sometimes when I need someone to talk
to, she will call at the right time.

My sister always tells me to keep on a prayer line,
never stop praying.

When we stop praying, that's when everything starts
to go wrong.

I will always remember my sister —the one person I
will always...*Love*.

My Brother

You have always been my brother;
You have always made us laugh;
You have always shown your strength, and we never see you cry.

Your children were always number one — your lifelong dream.

When your health was not at its best you changed your course of life. You made peace with the Lord and then you said goodbye.

Even though we miss you and wish that you had stayed,
We thank the Lord we had you here each and every day.

Comfort is My Wish

Courage is my prayer

H is for that first time that she holds me
O is when I opened my eyes and saw her
P is for her presence around me
E is for eternity, the life she will now live.

That was her hope for eternal life
No more pain, no more suffering and no more tears
She has gone to a better place of eternal life.

Thank you, Lord,

Thank you, Lord, for granting me life
Thank you, Lord, for granting me eyes to see
Thank you, Lord, for granting me a mouth,
with which to speak
Thank you, Lord, for granting me ears,
with which I hear
Thank you, Lord, for granting me feet,
that I can walk
I thank you Lord for everything
You are doing in my life.

At times I sit and wonder about these gifts.
What would my life have been like without them?
That is why I am thanking You Lord
for all the gifts in my life.

The Color of a Man's Skin

Why should the color of a man's skin determine if he can become wealthy or if he would become poor?

How does the color of a man's skin get to choose if he should eat or if he should starve?

Why does the color of a man's skin choose if he's right or if he's wrong?

Why must the color of a man's skin choose where he must reside and around whom?

How does the color of a man's skin get to choose if he should live or if he should die?

Why does the color of a man's skin choose if he can freely breathe the breath of life, or if someone will take it away from him?

Why should the color of a man's skin define his place in life?

When God created man, He never chose a color for his creation, so why is the color of a man's skin chosen for him today?

In God's domain all things were created equal!

The Gifts of Jehovah

Jehovah is the gift of abundant life.
Jehovah is the gift of unconditional love

Jehovah is the gift of sight
Jehovah is the gift of hearing
Jehovah is the gift of forgiveness
Jehovah is the gift of complete healing
Jehovah is the Heavenly gift and earthly peace
Jehovah is the gift that is given to all, that cannot be returned for a refund.

The most precious gift of Jehovah is the gift of everlasting life in eternity.

The Gifts of Yahweh

Yahweh is the gift of lives abundant.
Yahweh is the gift of
unconditional love.
Yahweh is the gift of sight.
Yahweh is the gift of hearing.
Yahweh is the gift of forgiveness.
Yahweh is the gift of healing.
Yahweh is the gift of peace.
Yahweh is the gift of mercy.
Yahweh is the gift of wisdom
and knowledge.
Yahweh is the gift of understanding.
Yahweh is the gift of blessing
and prosperity.
Yahweh is the gift of guidance
and protection.
Yahweh is the Heavenly gift
and earthly peace.
Yahweh is the gift that is given to each and every
person which cannot be returned for a refund.
The most precious gift of Yahweh is the gift of
everlasting life in eternity.

All these gifts are what Yahweh has for us on earth.

The Greatest Love

The greatest love is
falling in love with Jesus.
It is the love that fulfills your every desire and wish. He will never leave you, never hurt you nor will He forsake you or ever make you cry.

When you're hurting, He will comfort you, when you cry, He will wrap His arms around you and wipe away your tears. When you fall, He will pick you up and dust you off, making sure everything is alright with you.

A love like this is rare and very hard to find. A love like this is never lost — it lives on into eternity.

The Storm of Life

Read Matthew 7:25
Psalms 7:10-17
Ephesians 6:16

The storms of life are many and varied.
Abraham, Daniel, Jesus, and his disciples, all faced storms in their lives.

When we are in a storm some of us panic and sometimes it appears that when we call for help there is no one to help us. Yet, we only need to call on the name of Jesus who is our shield in time of storms.

Cry out Jesus save me (us)! If you trust in Jesus, Jesus is capable of calming the storm in your life.

Prayer
Lord, thank you that in all the storms of life I can cry out 'Lord, save me!' Help me to trust You in those times and not be afraid.

Through Your Eyes

Through their eyes I am no good, but through Your eyes, Jesus, I am good.
Through their eyes I am not worthy, but through Your eyes, Jesus, I am worthy.

Through their eyes I am unlovable, but through Your eyes, Jesus, I am loved unconditionally.
Through their eyes I am nothing, but through Your eyes, Jesus, I am awesome and wonderfully made.

Through their eyes I am untrustworthy, but through Your eyes, Jesus, I am honorable, dependable reliable, honest, and upright.

Through their eyes I am a failure, but through Your eyes, Jesus, I am victorious, blessed, and anointed.

Through their eyes I am scorned and cursed, but through Your eyes, Jesus, I am loved, my wounded heart is healed, I am adopted, chosen and destined.
I am redeemed, forgiven and free through Your blood that You shed for me.

A Tribute to my Mom
(Beryl Seales)

To my loving mother

Even though I did not get to grow up with you, I knew you had always loved me. At the age of ten years old you left me to be with the Lord and I was very hurt and angry with you for leaving me without saying goodbye, but I understand the reason today.

You were sick throughout your life's struggles and you ended up dying because you lacked the knowledge to take care of yourself. As a result of your death, I had to suffer for a while, until a guiding angel came and rescued me from the abuse I encountered because you were not there to protect me.

It was because of that guiding angel that I became the woman I am today. A loving, caring, compassionate and kindhearted person just as you were when you were alive.

At times when life became very challenging and difficult for me, I was very sad, because I needed my mom to hug me and to tell me that everything would be alright; but you were not there to comfort me.

Sometimes I sit and wonder what you would have become, and what accomplishments you would have made, if you had not died at such a young age.

I want to say thank you Mom, even though you were not here to see me grow up, and to witness my achievements, I am hoping that you are smiling down from Heaven with joy. Mama I just want to tell you that I love you and you're the queen of my heart. I just want you to know that loving you brings comfort to my soul.

I love you, Mom!

Today

Today I will say thank you to the Great I AM. He says to me, "Rise my child;" as He gently kisses my forehead, "today you have my work to do." As I rise in pain, I give Yahweh all praise, all glory and honor which belong to Him.

Today I will humble myself and try not to change or improve anyone other than myself.

Today I will improve my mind.
Today I will not find fault.
Today I will speak positive things
about my life and others.
Today I will do all things which are asked of me
from my Heavenly Father.

As the day ends, I hope that I accomplish all I intended to do…Today for my Jehovah.

Dedicated to
Glenda Yavette Lowman

Tomorrow

I am your tomorrow
What you can live and do today
Don't put off for tomorrow;
Tomorrow may be too late.

Who would have thought a friendly tap on the shoulder and there went my tomorrow?
Lying there in blood wondering will I live to see tomorrow?

All my dreams I've had today will they still be there…Tomorrow?

Who is going to tell my mother that her tomorrow has just died today!

Trust

The love that I trusted I have explored in my life.
I thought how much I knew me.

As I stand as if I were an ocean, deep and wide; as I gaze upon my heart seeing the surface of my soul; Judging only the face of my heart, body and soul Which I had made my shore, stretches far beyond.

I thought I was so great as I stand looking out onto the ocean of my soul. But someone was also looking at me. Then He called out to me and I came to Him in my surprise.

                It was the Lord.

Vacation

I thank you, Lord, for my vacation
which you approved for me—from November 16,
1962, into eternity.

Then I'll return home to You
and sit with You to tell You
all about my vacation (which you already know);
but I must still tell You all of what I did on my vacation
on earth.

The good things that I did, and even the not-so-good things too and why I did these things.

Before I was created You had an assignment for me, so You placed me in the womb of a woman called Beryl to carry me for nine months. After she had given birth to me, my life's journey began.

I had some joyous times, and I had some sad, sorrowful times, but through it all You have never left my side.

On January 1973 You called my mother home to be with You. As she departed, she kept her heart and mind on me, her only daughter, wondering what would become of her; but little did she know it was hell. But You, Lord, never abandoned me through it all.

You said that weeping will endure for a night, but joy will come in the morning; so I keep pressing on until my vacation on earth is over.

Then, I will return home to You to rest in Your arms in peace and quiet.

Wisdom

Wisdom is a key aspect of maturity; Wisdom grows when we learn to apply our knowledge to everyday choices and situations.

Wisdom comes from our relationship with God. No one needs to lack wisdom because God offers it freely to us when we ask.

As we seek God's wisdom, He will give us the opportunities to grow in our trust in Him, and that is when we begin to see His wisdom flourish in our lives.

As you ask God, who is more than willing to give you wisdom, to make you know how to live a Godly life through Him, transformation occurs. He transforms our old life into a new life by His grace.

Let me be eager to listen and discern Your voice. Grant me the desire to obey You so that when You speak, I will respond with joy-filled faithfulness. In Your name.

You Give Me Everything.

When I look back over my life and see the beauty of my life, Lord, You give me everything.

No one gives me life; no one gives me everlasting joy; no one gives me peace the way You can, and no one can comfort me the way You can. No one can love me unconditionally the way You do, despite my faults and all of my ways.

No one can protect me the way You can from harm and danger. No one can guide me in the ways You can, and no one will give their life for me like You did.

I Love You Lord.

What Is Love

Love is that feeling inside which
only one person can inspire;

Love is the feeling of fondness
Love is understanding each other
Love is sharing everything with each other

Love is that peaceful feeling you have in your heart
Love is giving all that you have inside to that person

Love is togetherness
Love is being there when he or she needs you

Love is everlasting.

Your Inspiration Journey

T - traveling through life journey with God, in this land of give-and-take

When sorrows and disappointments come in the storms of life, He embraced you in His arms.

H - His smiles —the way He wakes you up and gently holds your hands

Majestic and glorious are your works of art, and your wise designs are forever.

O - the omnipresence that is always around you in everything you do.

M - the memories of the fragrance of His love which you cannot forget, that sweet aroma in your spirit.

A - the way the Almighty calls you creative; your thinking ability for wisdom and success is the purpose you were call inspiration, hope, peace and tranquility in your life.

S - the seeds of your soul with wisdom that planted with faith growing strong as the oak.

Dreams

Don't bury your dreams in a place
called *'some day'*

Dreams give you energy and passion.
Dreams help you to believe in yourself.

Dig deep to reconnect with your dream
Because you have all it takes,

Live it, Learn it, Write it and Remember it!

Recapture your dreams — remember who you are in this life

Remember when you were a child, what you wanted to be, and the things you used to say.

With Almighty God, all things are possible!

So don't stop dreaming. With your Dreams you can change the world.

Who Am I

Some people call me black;
Which I am not.
Some people call me Negro;
Which I am not.
Some people call me African American;
Which I am not.
Some people call me colored;
Which I'm not.
Some people also call me nigger;
Which I'm not.

Let me tell you who I am!
I am the creation from eternity that came into time
Which my Heavenly Father made from the clay of the earth,
He took some light clay, then some dark clay; then he molded it and created me to be who and what I am.

So when people call me Black, Negro, African American, Colored or Nigger;
I wonder if they really know what those words mean;
But I'm still that child that God created in His own image and love.

In Loving Memory of
Betty Wilson

Sunrise 02/06/1938
Sunset 05/20/2007

B The beauty she had within her
E The energy she generated at all times
T The tenderness and love she showed to others
T The time and effort she took to help people.
Y The beautiful yesterdays we all shared with her

Betty:

The most beautiful, extraordinary, tender, loving person one could ever meet in this lifetime.

Now rest your head in your Father's arms and rest in peace.

In Loving Memory of
Minnie Wright

M - the memories she left behind
I - the incredible things she has done
N - the nobleness that resides within her
N - the nicest, kindest person anyone could encounter
I - the impossible things that she made possible
E - the eternal life she will now have with her Father in Heaven

In Loving Memory of
Olushola Franklyn-Williams

O	A voracious young king in his own way
L	Love and life experiences that he shared with everyone he met
U	Uniquely loved by everyone
S	A savior of souls in distress
H	Heroic in all aspects of his life
O	An over-achiever in everything that he did
L	The legacy of his life he left behind for all to learn from
A	An awesome savior to all who knew him

OLUSHOLA: A vibrant young king who left a legacy for us to live and learn by. You will be greatly missed.

In Loving Memory of
Dr. Rodolfo Lim

R- Respectful, radiant person he was. He touched so many lives with grace.

O- He overcame life's obstacles with patience, faith and hope.

D- He dedicated and embraced life with everyone he met.

O- His heart was an open door; he gave with courage and compassion.

L- The love he gave energized everyone he met and brought joy.

F- Faith and courage he gave to all. His were hands of comfort and love.

O- There was power in his life of beauty and grace that all could see.

L- The excellence of the light that shone when he walked into a room.

I- He inclined his heart to learn lessons of wisdom, and built understanding in hearts of others.

M- Memories of his journey will remain forever to all those he touched in his life.

Prayer
Lord, thank You that You are a shield, a savior, and a provider. Help me to keep trusting in You and not be afraid.
Help me to keep You as the number one priority in my life.

ABOUT THE AUTHOR

Monica Seales Thomas was born in the Republic of Trinidad and Tobago. She migrated to the United States of America in the year 1980, where she resided with her sister and family.

As a young girl, Monica would sit and write poems in her spare time. She had been writing for several years, stirred by the hurts and pains of life, and decided to put those feelings on pieces of paper as the years went by.

One day her sister noticed all her pieces of papers and suggested she put those poems in order and get them copyrighted and published.

That was the beginning of this collection of poems which has now taken shape. Today she is still writing, and her works are being revised and published.

www.ingramcontent.com/pod-product-compliance
Lightning Source LLC
Chambersburg PA
CBHW060854050426
42453CB00008B/977